# Feast or Famine?

Written by Sarah Irvine

Ireland

My name is Kieran. I live on a cattle farm near Tralee, in Ireland. My sister and I help lead the cattle to the fields where there is plenty of grass. It's hard work, but I love farming. What kinds of farms do you know about?

# Contents

Look for the **Activity Zone!**
When you see this picture, you will find
an activity to try.

# A Farming Country

The Republic of Ireland is farming country. A large part of the landscape is gently rolling lowlands, most of which is covered in grass. This kind of land is perfect for farming.

Farming is an Irish tradition that stretches back for centuries. Today, farms cover more than two-thirds of the country. Ireland's agricultural industries include raising livestock, such as cattle and pigs; producing dairy products; and growing crops such as potatoes, barley, and sugar beets.

agriculture   the science and practice of farming

# Irish Crops and Livestock

The Republic of Ireland is part of an island in northwest Europe.

Today, barley is Ireland's main crop. Barley is a grain, like wheat. It is used as animal feed and made into malt.

Cattle are often seen on Irish farms. Some are dairy cows, which are milked every day. Others are raised for beef.

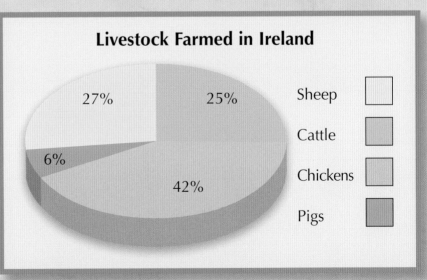

Livestock Farmed in Ireland

27%    25%
6%
42%

Sheep
Cattle
Chickens
Pigs

# The Emerald Isle

Ireland is often called the Emerald Isle, because its countryside is a rich green color. Ireland's climate helps produce good pastureland that is perfect for growing crops. The warm ocean currents in the Atlantic Gulf keep the winters mild and the summers cool. Grass stays green all year around because of the mild climate, and in many places livestock can eat grass, or graze, right through the winter. Ocean winds bring a great deal of rain to the island. On average, it rains about two days out of every three. However, parts of the west coast receive nearly three times as much rain as the east coast.

**pastureland**    land that is covered in grass for grazing animals

## Land Use in Ireland (Percentage)

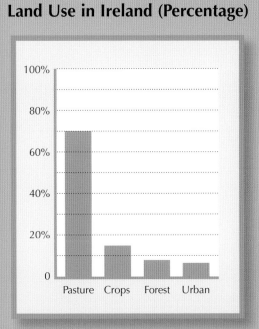

## Plenty of Rain!

The map below shows how much rain falls in each part of Ireland.

### Average Yearly Rainfall (Inches)

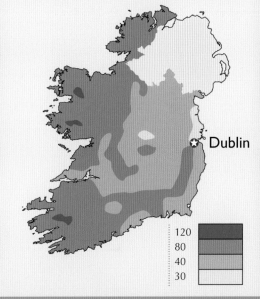

Dublin

120
80
40
30

Farmers in the southwest of Ireland have the longest growing season in the country. This region is warmer than anywhere else and very wet.

Dublin, the capital of the Republic of Ireland, is on the east coast, where it is the driest.

# Farming for Survival

Farming is one of the most important jobs in the world. Almost all the food that people eat comes from crops and animals raised on farms. Other products, such as wool, cotton, and leather, are also products of farming.

During the 1700s and 1800s, farming was the main way of life in Ireland, and most people lived on small farms. Usually the land did not belong to the farmers, however. They paid rent or gave part of what they grew to a local landowner. After growing enough crops and raising enough animals to feed their families, most farmers had nothing left over to sell. They were subsistence farmers.

subsistence farming  producing enough food for survival, with nothing left over for profit

8

Wealthy landowners lived in large country houses. They farmed some of their land and rented other parts to local farmers.

Poor farming people were known as *peasants*. Many found it hard to afford everyday items such as shoes, clothes, and tools.

Ireland has many rocks in its soil. In the past, farmers used the rocks to make walls to divide their land and hold in their animals. In many parts of Ireland, old stone walls are still used.

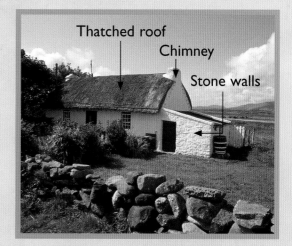

Thatched roof

Chimney

Stone walls

Farming families lived in small farmhouses called *crofts*. A croft had thick stone walls to keep out the cold in winter. It also had a stone fireplace and a thatched roof. Some families still live in crofts.

# Traditional Farming

During the 1700s, European farmers used old methods of farming that had been in place since medieval times. These systems were often inefficient. Some farms had little fencing, and animals often wandered into neighboring fields and ate the crops. Fields were left unplanted, or fallow, for a year after a crop was harvested so that the soil could recover its nutrients.

Wind and water were used to power some mills. However, the main power source was muscle power. Animals such as horses and oxen pulled plows. Farmers sowed seeds, harvested crops, threshed grain (separated the seeds from the straw), and cut firewood by hand.

inefficient   not efficient; wasteful of energy, time, or materials

# From a Lake to Peat

1. Shallow lakes formed during the Ice Age thousands of years ago. They slowly filled with mud.

2. Plants grew and died in these muddy bogs. The rotting vegetation sank to the bottom.

3. As the layers built up, a lack of air in the muddy water allowed only small plants such as mosses to grow.

4. Without air, the vegetation did not rot completely. Instead, it formed layers of peat, a soft, coal-like fuel.

Today, peat burning is restricted in many parts of Ireland, because it can pollute the air, and peat harvesting can harm wildlife.

For centuries, Irish farmers have cut peat from bogs to burn for cooking and heating. They have also used it to fertilize their fields.

# The Popular Potato

Potatoes were first brought to Ireland in the 1700s.
At first, farmers planted potatoes mainly because their
roots break up the soil, making it easier to sow grain.
However, potatoes soon became the main
crop and food for the Irish people.
They were easy to grow and very
productive. About 1.2 acres of land
planted with potatoes could feed
a family of six. Five times as much
land was needed to grow enough
grain to feed the same number
of people. Because potatoes
contain starch, protein, and many
different vitamins and minerals,
they are very nutritious.

The tubers are the parts
of the potato plant that
people eat. A tuber is a
swollen, underground stem
that stores food until the
next growing season.

starch   a type of food that provides a source of energy

The leaves make food for the plant using sunlight, water, and a gas in the air called *carbon dioxide*.

# Activity Zone!

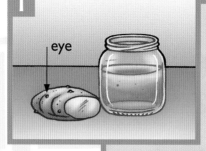

eye

1. Find a potato with plenty of eyes. Wash it and slice a little off one end. Find a jar wider than the potato. Fill it with water.

2. Stick toothpicks into the potato so that the half with the end sliced off rests in the jar. Make sure some eyes are in the water.

3. Keep the jar in a place with plenty of light but out of direct sunlight. Keep the water level close to the top of the jar. Watch for a couple of weeks. What happens?

Stems transport food from the leaves to the tuber. They also transport water from the roots to the leaves.

The roots take in water for the plant.

# The Great Famine

By the 1800s, potatoes were the only food for many
of the poor people in Ireland. Between 1845 and 1848,
Ireland suffered a major disaster when a plant disease,
called the *potato blight*, destroyed the potato crops.
These years became known as the Great Famine.
About one million people died from starvation
or disease; many more people left Ireland to seek
a better future in countries such as Australia,
Canada, and the United States.

During the famine, many
families lost their homes and
were forced to live in sod
houses dug into the earth. Laws
were passed to protect tenants'
rights, but it was many years
before the poverty eased.

When a farm or region grows only one crop, it is called a *monoculture*. This can be efficient if the crop is successful, but a problem with the crop can result in a disaster.

**efficient**   not wasteful of energy, time, or materials

By 1900, the population of Ireland was half of what it had been before the famine. Entire towns and communities no longer existed.

# The Importance of the Potato

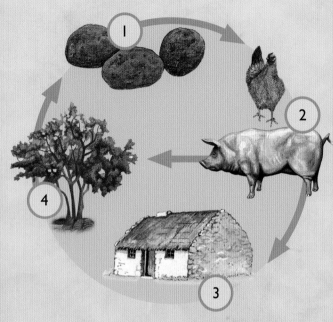

The potato was very important to the poor people in Ireland.

1. People ate the potato—the average person ate between 11 and 14 pounds of potatoes each day!

2. The skins and any tubers too small to eat were fed to pigs and chickens.

3. Pigs and chickens were sold to pay the rent.

4. The manure from the pigs was used as fertilizer to grow more potatoes.

# The Potato Blight

The potato blight that caused the Great Famine was a kind of fungus. The fungus's spores were carried from one plant to another by wind and water. The climate from 1845 to 1848 was perfect for spreading these fungus spores. It was particularly cool and damp.

The leaves are the first part of the plant to be attacked by the fungus. Black spots appear on the tops of the leaves, and a whitish mold grows underneath. The disease then travels down the stems and rots the potato tuber in the ground.

A farmer sprays potato plants to protect them from blight.

spore  a seedlike reproductive cell

The potato blight can still strike. Today, some farmers spray a chemical called a *fungicide* on their plants to kill the fungus.

Potatoes infected with blight

# Good and Bad Fungi

Many fungi produce chemicals that break down plant or animal cells so that the fungi can absorb their nutrients. Some fungi are important, because they break down dead matter. However, parasitic fungi, such as the potato blight, feed on and destroy living cells.

The potato blight can also infect tomato plants. Tomatoes and potatoes are related plants that both originated in South America.

# The Agricultural Revolution

Ireland was part of the agricultural revolution that transformed farming in Europe and America during the 1800s. Scientific advances made farming more productive.

- New farming tools and machines were invented to help farmers produce more.
- Improved breeding programs allowed farmers to increase the amount of meat their animals produced.
- New methods for growing crops were introduced. In each field, different crops were planted in sequence so that the nutrients taken out by one crop were returned by the next crop. A field never needed to lie fallow.
- Better fertilizers were developed.

fertilizer   a substance added to soil to help plants grow well

Scientists call crops such as clover and beans *legumes*. These crops add an important nutrient called *nitrogen* to the soil.

In the late 1700s, Englishman Robert Bakewell bred a new type of sheep that produced much more meat. Before that, most sheep were bred only for their wool.

# The Move to Mechanics

In about 1700, English farmer Jethro Tull invented the first farming machine with moving inner parts. It was a mechanical seed drill that made rows of small trenches in the soil and dropped seeds into them. It planted three rows at a time and used less seed than sowing by hand.

In the late 1800s, steam-powered threshers were invented to separate grain from straw.

# Farming Today

Today, most Irish people live and work in cities. Farming is now a career choice, not a necessary way of life. Many farmers specialize in certain types of farming, such as dairy farming or horticulture. Because of improved roads, farmers can easily transport their goods around the country. Furthermore, the invention of refrigeration has allowed them to export their products overseas.

Additionally, Ireland is now part of the European Union, a group of European countries that cooperate in areas such as politics and economics. These countries have shared agricultural policies and trade agreements. This makes it easier for Irish farmers to find buyers for their products.

**horticulture**   the science of growing fruits, vegetables, or flowers

Modern highways make it easy for trucks to carry goods from Irish farms to the Dublin docks, where they are shipped to the rest of Europe.

About a third of Earth's total land area is used for farming. That's about 12 billion acres!

# New Changes

It is important that countries consider the effects that farming has on the environment. In the past, the European Union encouraged farmers to produce as much food as possible.

## The Consequences
Farmers produced more food than was needed. This had some bad effects.

- Hedges were removed to create more farmland, which led to soil erosion.

- Marshy fields were drained, and more water was used for irrigation. This destroyed many wetlands.

- More chemicals were used to fertilize the soil and kill pests. This polluted ground water and rivers.

## The Solutions
The policies were changed. Farmers were paid to produce less on each piece of land, to plant trees, and to use fewer chemicals.

**environment** the surroundings in which a person, plant, or animal lives

# Botanists at Work

Scientists who study plants are called *botanists*. Their research can help farmers in many ways. Some botanists study soil nutrients and the best ways that farmers can keep their soil fertile to improve their crops. Other botanists study new methods of growing plants so that farmers can produce larger crops. Some carry out experiments to test the effects of chemical sprays. Other botanists study the genetic makeup of plants. They are always trying to find new ways to protect crops from diseases.

# DNA Detectives

A botanist works with potatoes.

Plants that have had their DNA altered to produce bigger crops or to resist disease are called *genetically engineered* plants. Some people argue about whether these plants are safe for humans to eat.

DNA material inside every plant or animal cell that contains information about what that plant or animal is like

Fungicides are expensive and can harm the environment if they are not used properly. Some botanists are trying to figure out ways of detecting the potato-blight fungus before it spreads. In 2000, two U.S. scientists took fungal DNA out of infected potato plants. They used this DNA to develop a test that will quickly identify the same DNA in other plants. If a potato sample is found to have fungal DNA, then the farmer knows it is infected.

23

# Find Out More!

1. What are some other mechanical inventions that changed farming?

2. What crops are farmed in your country? How have modern farming methods affected farming where you live?

To find out more about the ideas in *Feast or Famine?*, visit **www.researchit.org** on the web.

# Index